Balloon Animal

poems by

Chelsey van der Munnik

Finishing Line Press
Georgetown, Kentucky

Balloon Animal

Copyright © 2018 by Chelsey van der Munnik
ISBN 978-1-63534-531-5 First Edition
All rights reserved under International and Pan-American Copyright Conventions. No part of this book may be reproduced in any manner whatsoever without written permission from the publisher, except in the case of brief quotations embodied in critical articles and reviews.

ACKNOWLEDGMENTS

"[Minor]", "Test", & "Nobody" were previously published in Issue 104 of Right Hand Pointing, Nov 2016.
"Carrying" was previously published in BROAD! In Winter of 2015 as an "Untitled" poem.
"Out" was previously published in ZPlatt Literary/Arts Magazine in Spring 2015.
"Abort" was previously published in ZPlatt in Spring of 2014 under the title "Slip".

Publisher: Leah Maines
Editor: Christen Kincaid
Cover Art: Mikey Lemieux
Author Photo: Andrew Giroveanu
Cover Design: Elizabeth Maines McCleavy

Printed in the USA on acid-free paper.
Order online: www.finishinglinepress.com
          also available on amazon.com

Author inquiries and mail orders:
Finishing Line Press
P. O. Box 1626
Georgetown, Kentucky 40324
U. S. A.

Table of Contents

Young Girl

Part I: Blowing Up
It Happens 1
Abort 2
[Youth] 3
Test 4
[Minor] 5
My Daddy 6
My Mommy.. 7

Part II: Expanding
How My Body Will Always Be Yours 9
Risk, Release 10
Trying To Save Me... 11
[The Obsolete Man] 12
How Creation Makes You Useless....................................... 13
Nobody 14
Reach, Feel... 15
[Older] 17
How Who You Are Can Be Hidden 18
Replay I 19
[Amniocentesis] 20
My Early Was a Baby.. 21

Part III: Untying
Brim.. 22
[See It No Other Way] 23
Carrying.. 24
Balloon Animal... 25
[Milked] 26
Out.. 27
How We Dig Up Our Own Remains 28
Replay II... 29
My Name is Trauma 30
Replay III 31

Young Girl

A young girl, let's say, who can't hug her father.
And her mother, for instance, looking only to God.
Ignoring obvious signs of future derailment
in a young girl to seek her own peace, praying
for God to do something for the girl while giving up,
turning away.

The older boy with no need for protection.
A young girl seeing love in the bare skin of it all.
Now, a young girl is pregnant and ruined in a way
only unexpecting and unlikely mothers can fully
understand.

[the child, the blessing.]
Why can't the young girl see her mother's God?

Part I: Blowing Up

It Happens

I only missed my period by one day or so, but I knew in that instance.
My body pleading in a way to stop torturing it by staying with the guy—just
take this baby and run. After I found out how far along I was,
I traced conception back to a moment on his father's couch—a blanket
over us, his father in the chair next to us. I don't think either of us
even enjoyed the sex, but putting his dick in me was a necessity
when we were together. He would pull out before something came out.
I guess he forgot that time.

Abort

Mom, can I talk to you?

Every sentence an unmapped quest into the woods.
the end of my sentence somehow misplaced on the other side,
my crumb-trail to start over gobbled by sparrow beaks.
What have I even said so far? Now I've gone too far, I'm lost.

Leaves brush my cheeks, comforting my forgetfulness.
Mounds of buried prose. Collapsing resting stones lined up,
sentence Lost, conversation Lost. A family of died-at-births.

Words stack on words, piling too high, covered in chunky moss,
becoming meaningless, fruitless in dry earth, trampled.
I can't always be there to catch pieces fall, dig them up, or revivify.

My tongue seizes in the fever of the lush forest.
Swamp gums slipping on teeth tombstones, falling out one by one.
Throat gasping, clawing at thick air to complete the idea.

To catch the thoughts slithering through furtive trapdoors.
To untangle my phrases from espaliers, rose bushes, maple sap,
To try to pluck them out of rabbit holes, the mouths of snakes,
bear traps with silver teeth.

What is it?

I…forgot what I wanted to say.

[Youth]

Sturdy branch
Really not

Going fast
For them

The night
Of wings

That face
She said
An angel

Curtains close
Footprints rove

Other ocean
Invisible bells

A razor
Never fair

But yes
Always yes.

Test

This piss covered stick is my loaded gun
Two pink lines making two bleeding holes

One in my mother who saw it coming
And turns her nose up
One for my father, clueless and crying
And trying to hug it out

I suppose I knew I would kill them this way

[**Minor**]

guilt
arrives as
prison dust

[wait to
escape]

swallow
all of it

grain by
grain

My Daddy

the plainest green of a small town day
he's overcast but not quite raining yet.

a brown belt around his mashed potato belly
and the crack of a can of Pepsi—
man spreading on his living room couch

a yawning fifty year old with a pen in hand—
how much should I make the check out for?

My Mommy

back to me at the kitchen counter,
you never seem to look my way.

I hear sewing, you putting together
each piece of carefully selected

fabric. an unreadable map,
you are uncharted territory.

your eyes direct like a pitch
black sky, I can never

get a sense of who you are.

no light or breath
to form myself. save the smell

of a candle. or the color of your hair
on the back of your head.

Part II: Expanding

How My Body Will Always Be Yours

prop on a stage
re-usable space

eyes to the raised floor
greeting the onlookers tour

not for you so give it up
a sight to see with

none of the glory
time passes—still feels the same.

Risk, Release

Talk to the arm of captivity
because you'll find its your own
hand that bends, opening and closing

speaking in a frustrated tone
slapping your bald face hard
waiting for you to bark

an unlikable acrobat
wriggling away from reality

you are a greedy dreamer
now beyond quarantine

give birth the bug
risk your kingdom
be released from yourself

Trying To Save Me

a boy named Sam
with glossy brown eyes
a head of red hair.

he stood, waving me out
of the math class i was in.
i asked to go to the bathroom,
only to stand in the hall
in the sunlight of having
my pregnant body accepted.

Sam liked to touch my belly, he'd smile,
I was human to him.

He had wanted to date me
but i turned him down
to pursue the older guy,
the guy who would put

a baby in me.

[The Obsolete Man]

too local a fire
sense the heat   not permitted
walk away   plodding
this water hurting   a snake enfolding
narrowing around   muscles

my body   gasp striking
still an open doorway
we don't really like this, right?
heaviness   fingertips   welts   creation
your arm deep   shouting cool sweat

sour breath   that middle
sleep   guessing but knowing
misplace all toenails
one   aching boot   and still
deserve your   lack

knowing   not refreshing
make me   care   to rip
unfolding hair   out around
lesser wrists   tread I may
kick you   sad   near fire

nudge you   right in
toes nothing   my boots down
on them   uncluttered eyes   change.

How Creation Makes You Useless

Just a stray cat of a belly.
No one really wants to look.

Certainly, no one wants to touch
[don't want to get fleas.]

The stray cat belly looks away,
tries to hide, turns its nose up

thinks its better than you
even if its hideous to look at.

Happy on its own, don't you worry.
But actually kind of starving.

A little cold. Maybe sort of lonely.
But never mind that. This stray cat belly

wants you to stay away [it's not hungry]
never wanted your look or touch

in the first place.

Nobody

wants
to touch
a pregnant
fourteen
year old's
belly.

Reach, Feel

you reach, you feel
a velvet stone in the bottom of a bag

deep in a foxhole
a trinket under a dusty bed

way back in the corner
reachable if you strain, stretch

a coconut high in the tree
only the tips of your fingers can graze

maybe it's a smooth
piece of produce at the store

one you slip your
fingers over as you pass

skin firm to press,
wet from the sprinklers

one you're not interested in having
but desperately wish to experience

its inside of you
you can't do anything about it

it pushes, its hard
its heavy all over

a human head of a thing
at the end of the hall

it's a crowded, packed closet
of gray and white matter

a low frequency hum in your body

you only just realized as it moved

it's a baby in
you

[Older]

That house
So pale
Her wilderness

The flames
Come again
Be known

Make us
Our skin
Not safe

Boy's face
Sharpened tools
Cold sky

Better run
Never ask
You're right

How Who You Are Can Be Hidden

tiny, greasy, teenage face
embodiment of tears
eager to be older

nearer than imaginable to ruin
moving through a foggy reality
opening up to the wrongness

mess-up, screw-up, stupid girl
so blind
trauma brewed like the flu

eager to be older
running from being small
eyes won't meet yours

open arms won't be for you
trapped in uneducated lust
you did it, you know it

pressed forever into the mold
ever a stupid slut.

Replay I.

I was hit in the back of the head, the round, jutting out bit.
But not really. Just fertilized by a lying boy. Jutting in front.
I'd wake up forgetting I was in such a state of look awayness.
I was high on it because in forgetting the unhappiness, I could
seem strong; *look how she holds her chin up.* But I was only
refusing to look down.

[Amniocentesis]

Drag around
Your heavy peace

Keeping time
Minutes fly

Up ahead
Much pain
Give it up

She saw
A needle
An answer

With red
Hold it

This cell
That cage
Home still alive

Mother's faith
As rain

As swift rays
Swallowed us

And kept
My sameness.

My Early Was a Baby

my young was not too womb
because it accepted, allowed growth
without my consent
the wind plants seeds in the fertile
yet unknowing soil

my wrongness was way too life
it isn't natural for a child to have a child
a child to have a child
everyone made sure i knew
what my body was doing was ugly

who is chance to have this me?
the deservedness of it makes me sick
a guilt i've chosen, that's chosen me back

continuing in wrapping questions
like a newborn's blanket swaddling
or that seed returning
to the ground, building itself a separate
tree and strengthening, turned

deliberately away.

Part III: Untying

Brim

rotten pumpkin hole with string guts sun drying out
bloated cow belly busting along some unseen seam

the grass is chewed too long then puked as wet pages
water that fills a cup in a round, wiggling meniscus

sucking helium into this balloon, filling with dizziness
pop thats only a puff of maybe air. no one heard it

dirt moving beneath a snake digesting a pink mouse
the sound of roots grabbing soil as their own. they can

only come out by ripping them up, the cow's insides
can only be seen once its dead. humming dead bowels

the smiling pumpkin decay. spilling, spilling, spilling
tip over the cup and let it out, let it go. here it comes

[See It No Other Way]

Your object
My crown
Almost here

Draws blood
With ideas
Almost here

Breathless question
My mouth
And two

Bruised knees
Before me
I can

Be judged
Like you
And dream

A movie
Dull lives
It dies

Carrying

She preferred one side of my stomach like the
indented side of a king bed, making me a
deflating soccer ball, but smaller. I could only
fit a tiny carry-on, an efficient young womb only
hungering the smallest portions. When she
wanted out early in the middle of the night,
I reached between my legs and her head was
fuzzy and hard, feeling only as big as a lemon.
Big. She will make her way. What seemed slight
inside needs so much room to come out.

Balloon Animal

these marks spread skin ready to spread more
a thinning head of hair more skin stronger shredding

don't scratch my belly afraid of catching a nail
on scar tissue ripping out intestines stretching

accidentally touch heart grows fat pulling finger feels
changed skin stays long the fingertip buzzing

belly button tied up ready to untangle spray
moist air out a balloon let go around a room

my eye shaped marks   what they've seen cry a bit
blink it away let it gloss over blood shot

they speak like small but loud mouths
Feel me, I am strength.

skin asked to do more than it truly can
move to new cities for someone else

spread way too thin taut a balloon blown biggest
even when this thing is out, I can't go back to

being me.

[Milked]

Exhale of pleasure
        an exhale of death
a final happy breath
        [Release of pressure]

Then one to two
        a then and now
your final solo bow
        [Must love on cue]

Your arms aren't yours
        break them up
you are only the cup
        [They're the one
                that pours]

Out

blow out a candle
smoke stepping stairs to ceiling
I wish to escape up, away, vanish
empty eddying white fog

How We Dig Up Our Own Remains

such a deep ignorance that
I'm forced to revelation:

a bee forced to love
a blossom—I must believe

I'm not ruining each moment
by constantly looking away

staying in the bed
I've made warm.

hot holding bedroom air
[lord] keep my freedom

so I still have something
to lose: a sip, a bottle—

means nothing when each
day is wet and gone

like mushed paper in
the gutter. No one believes

how lost I was when I
found the key in my guts.

Replay II.

I was pregnant with amnesia. My placenta was trauma, my tiny womb held a blackout, my eyes saw nothing. I was recording the whole time but the lens cap was on. I replay the moments looking for a seam where some light can pass in and allow remembrance to settle the stomach ache sort of depression still there. I just want a peek to piece any two parts together. I zoom in and allow the lens to jut out so far that it cracks the glass. Still nothing.

My Name is Trauma

you still can't look right at me
but i stare right at you.

listen to my voice. i made you
unsure. you forgot how to respond

you think back on the whole situation
as being [not that bad]. that was me.

attacking your memory
gave me great joy
i smuggled moments away

but then they just followed
willingly after a while,

[Stockholm Syndrome.
happens a lot]

what reason did i have?
it's simple. you could not
[cannot] handle that kind of

body bastardization.

Replay III.

They're almost happy memories, but their landing is a horrific crash. I don't remember speaking much, I don't remember my body, I don't remember many emotions. I remember straightening my hair every morning, putting on a little makeup. I remember eating two lunches from the cafeteria each day. I remember her moving in my belly, thinking that was pretty cool. These notes along a skinny clothesline, pinching harder than any pain of emptiness because they're almost happy memories.

Chelsey grew up in Northeast, New York. At fifteen, she gave birth to her daughter, Lydia—the emotions and moments surrounding this event being the subject of *Balloon Animal*.

She later attended SUNY Plattsburgh where she double majored in Poetry and Psychology.

Her work has been published in *ZPlatt Literary Magazine, Crack The Spine, BROAD!, Poetry Super Highway,* and *Right Hand Pointing*.

www.ingramcontent.com/pod-product-compliance
Lightning Source LLC
LaVergne TN
LVHW041600070426
835507LV00011B/1202